THE REI REMODEL GUIDEBOOK

A SIMPLE STEP-BY-STEP PROCESS TO SAVE TIME AND MONEY WHILE REMODELING INVESTMENT PROPERTIES

"I have known DC for nearly two decades, and this book is an encapsulation of his expertise. His dedication to helping others is commendable."

—HRATCH YACOUBIAN, Real Estate Investor

"DC Cayce is the real deal! He has done remodeling from both sides—as a contractor and investor. This gives him a unique perspective that is both fresh and insightful. Do not be fooled—the remodel process can be a nightmare for a homeowner or the difference between making a profit or a loss on an investment property. And this is precisely why DC's book detailing the remodel process is a must-read!

—DAN RUDAT, Investor and CEO, CREI

"The key to building wealth in real estate investments is not just buying right; it is also rehabbing right! DC Cayce gives you the tools to have a successful remodel.

"There is an old saying in the construction industry: 'You don't get what you expect but what you inspect.' This book teaches you how to make sure you get what you expect in a timely and cost-effective way. This book is a must-read for new investors and will save you from costly overruns and construction delays.

"DC Cayce has made rehabbing property easier and less confusing. I highly recommend this book to anyone interested in buying investment real estate properties or rehabbing their personal home."

—**NORMAN HENRY**, Investor and Congressional Award Recipient for Community Development

"*The REI Remodel Guidebook* unpacks a simple step-by-step process for the person hungry to understand and implement real estate investment principles. This guidebook does an impeccable job of creating a sense of urgency; again, I say, it is a must-read."

—**JEREMIAH FLOWERS**, Founder and CEO, www.TaxNerd.us

"Phenomenal guide to remodeling your investment property. This book shares not only the experience and knowledge of an accomplished remodeler but also his everyday procedures and forms. Most books focus on the big picture and leave out the nitty-gritty details. The info in this book helped me to plan ahead and keep my budget on track, even when I ran into a few hiccups along the way. DC comes from a family of builders and investors. His expertise is second to none."

—**Ethan Stangl**, Investor, Realtor, and Property Manager

"Follow *The REI Remodel Guidebook* only if you desire to earn more thousands of dollars and save hundreds of hours of frustration. Trust me—if I had a copy of DC's guidebook years ago, I might have stayed in the home construction & improvement business!

—**Dr. Jim Harris**, Advisor to Leaders and Former Home Building Executive

THE REI REMODEL GUIDEBOOK

A SIMPLE STEP-BY-STEP PROCESS TO
SAVE TIME AND MONEY WHILE
REMODELING INVESTMENT PROPERTIES

DC CAYCE

HIGH BRIDGE BOOKS
HOUSTON

The REI Remodel Guidebook
by DC Cayce

Printed in the United States of America
ISBN: 978-1-954943-18-6

High Bridge Books titles may be purchased in bulk for educational, business, fundraising, or sales promotional use. For information, please contact High Bridge Books via www.HighBridgeBooks.com/contact.

Published in Houston, Texas by High Bridge Books

CONTENTS

INTRODUCTION

If you are reading this book, you probably know all too well that remodeling an investment property is not as easy as they make it look on television.

Are you seeking a better way to remodel? This book will show you how to remodel differently.

Hello, my name is DC Cayce, and I have made it my mission to help you take control of your remodel by helping you master the two key ingredients of a successful remodel: your budget and schedule.

There are several other ingredients to a successful remodel, and we will cover those as well. However, if your remodel were a recipe, the two main ingredients would be the budget and schedule.

As a direct result of trial and error (mine and others), *The REI Remodel Process* was created.

I have been on both sides of the REI remodel—as a contractor working for investors and as an investor with contractors working for me.

I worked for myself and for corporations—as a contractor, as an investor, and as an employee who managed real estate assets. I have trained contractors, construction workers, and real estate investors.

While completing hundreds of investment projects, I realized the remodel is the hardest thing to control.

Working with contractors who know nothing about real estate investing will make you want to pull your hair out!

Have you heard the phrase "you make your money when you buy your investment property"? That is true; however, you can easily lose it when you remodel through mismanagement of the budget and schedule.

This book will help you minimize your risk while you maximize your profit through streamlining the remodeling process.

You will be using proven planning and management methods that are simple to apply.

Stay in control of your project and keep your contractors in check by following the process.

Save yourself the expected headaches that come along with remodeling investment properties.

Say it with me…

No more headaches!

The REI Remodel Process has three different stages:

1. Pre-Remodel (plan),
2. Mid-Remodel (manage)
3. Post-Remodel (prepare for listing)

I will walk you through each stage and, at the end of each chapter, include images of the first page of all the forms mentioned and used during the process.

At the end of this introduction is the *REI Remodel Checklist,* which will help guide you through the steps of *The REI Remodel Process.*

Please visit www.reiremodel.com/forms to get the free PDF downloads.

I am here to help guide you through a successful remodel. If you have any questions, please email me at dc@reiremodel.com, or reach out to me on Instagram @reiremodel.

REI Remodel Checklist Property: 1234 Remodel St.

	Stage 1: Pre-Remodel	
	Step	**Notes**
☐	1. Schedule utilities	Water: Power: Gas:
☐	2. Secure property/ change locks	
☐	3. Property analysis	As-is value: Rehab cost: Arv: Rent:
☐	4. Selling or leasing?	
☐	5. Walk property with *Scope Sheet & QC Checklist*	
☐	6. Complete remodel scope	
☐	7. Establish final budget	
☐	8. Contact contractor(s)	
☐	9. Walk the project with contractor(s) and review *Scope Sheet*	
☐	10. Receive bids from contractor(s)	
☐	11. Select contractor(s)	
☐	12. Discuss pay arrangements and project schedule with contractor(s)	
☐	13. Complete design selections	
☐	14. Order design selections	
☐	15. Give detailed design selections to contractor(s)	
☐	16. Submit plans for permitting (if necessary)	
☐	17. Complete final schedule and confirm with contractor(s)	
☐	18. Talk to neighbors	
☐	19. Ready to start the project!	

1

PART 1

PRE-REMODEL

The Pre-Remodel is where we put the remodel plan together. We will cover the game plan, choosing contractors, design selections, establishing your final budget, permitting, scheduling, and everything else in between. To manage any project effectively, we need a well-thought-out plan to execute.

1

GAME PLAN

Planning is the only way to ensure a successful remodel.

Whether you are selling or leasing your property, you need to make an efficient exit to maximize your profit. Creating a game plan is the foundation of every remodel and will guide you toward success.

Once you get the keys to your new investment property, turn the utilities on and complete an inspection.

Use the included *Scope Sheet* and *Quality Control Checklist* to determine the scope of work needed for your project.

You may give these sheets to contractors to help them bid on your project. They will also help you identify big-ticket items to address, such as:

- Foundations
- Sub-floors
- Roofs
- Sewer lines
- Septic tanks
- Mold removal
- Chimneys
- Plumbing
- Windows
- HVAC
- Electrical systems
- Water damage

One of the first things you want to do is check all systems to identify if they are in good working condition (plumbing, sewer, electrical, and HVAC).

Get reports or certifications for these items to give potential buyers peace of mind about the condition of your property and to help escrow progress smoothly.

After you find out what needs repair, evaluate your property. Does it need:

- Freshening up?
- An update?
- A complete remodel?

Consider the largest selling features of your property—the kitchen and master bathroom. Also, take into consideration separate work areas and offices for potential buyers who work from home.

You may do an evaluation and find that you only need to do simple upgrades that will provide good returns and help your house sell faster, such as:

- Painting
- Flooring
- Fixtures
- Lighting placement
- Designer touches

While creating your game plan, do not forget your curb appeal! Think of cost-effective ways to enhance your landscape.

REI REMODEL TIP: At the beginning of a remodel, plant grass seed instead of new sod so it has time to grow and is ready when it is time to sell or lease.

If you are planning on selling your property, the scope of your project will vary greatly from a lease scope.

For leases, you may want to repair and refinish as many items as possible, whereas to sell, you may need to upgrade most items.

Always check to see what can be salvaged and will compliment your game plan, regardless of your exit strategy.

While planning, it is a good idea to make a priority list of wants versus needs. You can quickly free up budget space in case of an unforeseen problem during your remodel. (I wish problems never occurred, but hey, this is remodeling!)

Use the *Scope Sheet* to take notes and record quantities or measurements.

Use the *Quality Control Checklist* to assist you while inspecting the property to create the project scope.

The *Quality Control Checklist* will help you circumvent common issues that could delay escrow closing—if you are selling the house, of course.

What improvements are necessary to sell or rent your property?

Do not assume you need to complete a full remodel. However, do not under-improve your property either.

I know you have reviewed comps to make your purchase, but look again, this time with your mind focused on remodeling.

- What sells?
- What are the average days on market (DOM)?
- What kind of remodel is needed to sell or rent quickly?

Determine what is needed and then evaluate your budget. You already have an estimated idea of the cost to remodel, but now is the time to tighten it up.

Are you new to managing projects? If so, it may seem difficult to come up with a realistic budget. Several resources can help you get tighter ballpark figures before meeting with contractors.

Look at the following three sites for good ideas on pricing:

1. homewyse.com,
2. fixr.com/costguides.html,
3. homeadvisor.com/cost.

Some possible costs you do not want to overlook are:

- Changing the locks
- Building permits
- Inspections (sewer, septic, foundation, HVAC, electrical, plumbing, termite, chimney, pool, well)
- Cleaning
- Yard maintenance
- Pro photos
- Staging
- Appliances

- Wireless security system

For approximate pricing on these items, call the individual contractors and the building department to receive permitting fees (or look online).

Once you have gone through these steps, commit to your game plan, establish your budget, and stick to it!

Include at least a 15% contingency for unforeseen expenses.

In case of emergency, be adaptable. Issues often occur (hopefully small ones), but being adaptable will allow you to handle them quickly and effectively. If you must make cutbacks, focus on the items that will give you the highest return.

RECAP

- Inspect your property to get a good scope of work.
- Ask yourself, "What work is necessary to sell or rent in this neighborhood?"
- Create a ballpark budget before reaching out to contractors.

Quality Control Checklist

Property: 1234 Remodel St.

Yes	No	N/A	Answer Yes Or No To Each Of These Items
			Utilities
✓			Water is on
✓			Power is on
	✓		Gas is on
	✓		All gas appliances are lit (stove, water heater, etc)
			Exterior
			General
	✓		Doors open and close correctly
	✓		Paint is 100% complete (no peeling, mold, etc.)
✓			All stucco or siding is intact
	✓		Dry rot or termite damage has been replaced or repaired (fascia, eaves, etc.)
	✓		Exterior outlets are GFCI and enclosed in a waterproof housing
	✓		Exterior doors have weather stripping and thresholds installed correcty
✓			Doorbell works
✓			Mailbox is installed
	✓		Address numbers are installed and correct
✓			Exterior hose bibs do not leak and operate correctly
✓			Exterior lighting have bulbs and are operable
			Landscaping
	✓		Lawn sprinklers function correctly and are on an automatic timer
	✓		Landscaping is complete, grass is cut, and lawn maintenance is scheduled
✓			All fencing is upright and gates operate correctly
	✓		Trash bins are placed neatly inside garage or on the side of the house
	✓		All trash and remodeling materials have been hauled away
			Pool
		✓	Pool has been cleaned and is on a maintenance schedule
		✓	Pool equipment is in working condition (pump, filter, timer, light, and heater)
		✓	A GFCI plug has been installed for the pool equipment
		✓	Fencing and gates have been installed around the pool as needed
			Interior
			General
	✓		Smoke detectors are installed on each floor of the home, in every bedroom, and outside all sleeping areas
	✓		Carbon monoxide detectors are installed on each floor of the home, within 15 ft of each every bedroom
	✓		All light fixtures and ceiling fans are functioning correctly and have light bulbs installed

GAME PLAN

Scope Sheet

Address: 1234 Remodel St, AnyCity, USA

Bed/ Bath: 4/3 **SqFt:** 2300 **Year:** 1983

Exterior		
Stucco- 2'x2' patch	Siding/ Fascia- repair 16'	Brick- NA
Roof- good	Patio- good	Landscape- cleanup
Fence- replace (6) 6" pickets	Concrete- repair cracks	Foundation- good
Crawlspace- good	Garage- new door & opener	Pool/ Spa- NA
House #s- replace (12345)	Mailbox- good	Other-
Electrical		
Panel- upgrade	Wiring- good	Exhaust Fan- install (2)
Gfci- install (4)	Plugs- replace	Switches- replace
Smokes- 6	CO- install (2)	Doorbell- replace
Bulbs- 16	Other-	Other-
Fixtures		
Ext. Ceiling- 1	Ext. Wall- 5	Entry- retrofit recessed (1)
Living- fan	Family- fan	Den- NA
Dining- chandelier	Kitchen- (6) 6" recessed lights	Halls- retrofit recessed (4)
Master bed- fan	Bed2- flush mount	Bed3- flushmount
Bed4- NA	Bed5- NA	Master bath- vanity lights (2)
Bath2- vanity light (1)	Bath3- vanity light (1)	Bath4- NA
Other-		
Plumbing		
Water Heater- replace	Re-pipe- NA	Relocate- washer & dryer
Hose bibs- no leaks	Angle valves- replace (12)	Faucet Lines- replace (12)
Toilets- replace (3)	Kit.Sink- new	Bath Sink- new (4)
Kit.Faucet- replace	Bath Faucets- replace 4 in (4)	Tubs- replace tub (1)
Shower Pan- build (2)	Garbage disposal- replace	Kit.Drain- replace
Bath Drains- new shower (2)	Shower Trim- new	Shower Valves- replace (3)
Gas Valves- good	Other-	
HVAC		
System- works	Thermostat- replace	Registers- replace (9)
Service- yes	Swamp Cooler- NA	Other-
General Rehab		
Demo/ Haul- full demo	Framing- NA	Drywall- repair
Trashout- need 40 yard (1)	Other-	
Doors/Windows/Trim		
Ext.Doors- keep	Patio Doors- replace 72" slider	Int.Doors- replace (2)-32"
Windows- repair (2)	Ext.Knobs- replace (2)	Int.Knobs- 10
Hinges- replace (20)	Door Stops- install (10)	Shower Doors- install 60" (2)
Base- install 326 LF	Casing- replace 124 LF	1/4 Round- NA
Other-		
Paint		
Ext.Body- paint	Ext.Trim- patch & paint	Fence- paint
Int.Walls/ Trim- paint (3) colors	Cabinets- NA	Concrete- NA
Other-		

Project Budget

Property: 1234 Remodel St.

Major Systems			
System	**Description**	**Ballpark $**	**Final $**
Septic System	NA	NA	
Sewer	Needs inspection	$300	
Roof	Good. Get roof cert from roofer	$150	
HVAC	Needs service	$250	
Electrical Panel/ System	Upgrade	$3000	
Water Heater	Replace existing	$800	
Windows	Repair (2) windows	$300	
Plumbing System	Copper pipes in good shape	NA	
Foundation	No issues	NA	
Siding/ Stucco	Good shape	NA	
Chimney/ Fireplace	Functional	NA	
Crawlspace	No issues	NA	
Termite/ Pest Control	Exterminate roaches	$200	
Pool Spa	NA	NA	
Well	NA	NA	
Misc			

General Remodel			
Item	**Description**	**Ballpark $**	**Final $**
Lock Change/ Trashout	Change exterior locks. 40 yd trash out	$1650	
Demo	Whole house. Need additional 40 yd dumpster	$2500	
Framing/ Insulation	NA	NA	
Doors/ Windows	Replace (2)-32" int	$400	
Drywall	Patching throughout	$1950	
Paint	Complete interior/ exterior	$9300	
Kitchen	All new	$10,000	
Bathroom(s)	All new. (2) guest, (1) master	$18,000	

2

CHOOSING CONTRACTORS

Do not rush to pick contractors. Take the time to choose the right ones.

Choosing contractors is the most critical decision of your remodel. A bad contractor will completely derail your project, so do your due diligence in selecting them.

Do not rush through this step!

Even if you do the labor yourself, you will need some professional help—especially if work needs to be done to the systems (plumbing, electrical, HVAC).

Select the right contractor for the right job.

I usually use multiple contractors, but if you are just starting to manage your own projects, you might want to consider using a general contractor (GC). I tend to use one main contractor to handle general items such as:

- Demo
- Painting
- Installing fixtures
- Tile work
- Fencing
- Carpentry
- Drywall repair
- General repairs

And the following contractors for specialty items:

- Plumber
- Electrician
- HVAC tech
- Flooring installer
- Cabinet/countertop installer
- Window installer
- Landscaper
- Roofer
- Garage door installer
- Pool guy
- Tub reglazer

Also, make sure to have backup contractors in case you replace the one you decided to work with.

WHERE TO FIND CONTRACTORS

When first starting out, finding good contractors is not easy. It is a process, and you may need to go through a few before finding ones that stick.

A good contractor or team of contractors is critical to your success. Review the following ways to get started on the right foot.

1. Ask friends, family, and neighbors for referrals.

I suggest you start here; referrals are by far the best way to find good contractors. They have already been tested, and you have a better idea of who you are dealing with.

2. Ask your local investment group.

You cannot go wrong with referrals from fellow investors. If a contractor performed well for another contractor, they likely will for you as well, but do not let your guard down with any referral. Always complete your due diligence.

3. Ask material suppliers.

Suppliers may be able to give you contacts, but keep in mind that they sell materials. They do not necessarily see the materials installed or know how they were installed. They might like a contractor, but that does not mean he/she is the right one for you.

4. Google

I am sure it does not surprise you that Google is a great source for reviews. You can see a contractor's online presence and the especially important testimonials.

5. Search contractor vetting websites.

Sites like Angie's List and HomeAdvisor provide information about contractors, pictures of their work, testimonials, and ratings from customers they have worked with.

6. Place an ad.

I have done this several times with success. I have placed online ads and used the *Contractor Worksheet* to qualify them.

7. Check contractors buying supplies at material suppliers.

Whenever I go to material supply stores, I keep a lookout for contractors. I notice the way they talk and carry themselves, and then I engage in conversation about the work they do. I have found a few good contractors this way.

HOW TO QUALIFY CONTRACTORS

So you have found some candidates—what now?

Use the *Contractor Worksheet* to start calling and interviewing them via phone.

Did they answer when you called or call you back in a timely manner?

If you have not checked already, also look for online reviews.

Below are interview questions that I suggest asking contractors:

1. Are you licensed and insured?
2. How long have you been remodeling homes?
3. How many homes have you remodeled?
4. Do you have references I can contact?
5. Can I see past work you have completed?
6. Will you have a dedicated crew working on my property until completion? How many workers will be dedicated to my project?
7. How will the project be supervised?
8. How do you communicate with clients?
9. Will you obtain all the necessary permits?
10. What is your typical payment schedule?

11. How long do you think it would take you to complete this type of project?

12. Can you describe your typical workday?

13. What is your availability? How many projects do you have going on right now? How many can you handle?

14. How do you handle change orders?

15. Will you provide a written lien waiver?

For each trade, interview as many contractors as you can.

This is a simple process, and you will be able to weed through some contractors quickly with the provided questions.

If you are unable to manage all trades, look for a general contractor.

Keep in mind, a GC will charge an additional fee on top of the subcontractor cost as compensation to schedule and manage them.

Once you have narrowed down your choices, schedule an on-site meeting with the contractors to receive a bid.

REI REMODEL TIP: Know what you need before getting bids, and let contractors know you know what you need via your Scope Sheet.

Ask for a ballpark figure based on the scope you gave them just to get an idea of their prices. I like doing this to help condition the contractors on the pricing I am looking for and save them time if they are way out of range.

I once had a contractor give me a ballpark price of $50,000 for a 1400 square foot home we were just going to clean up and paint. Our budget was $15,000! And no, this property was not in Beverly Hills.

That contractor was not compatible with our objective. The fancy car he drove up in also gave me a hint of what he would charge.

During and after meeting potential contractors, ask yourself the following questions:

- Did they show up on time for the walkthrough?
- Did they deliver the bid when they said they would?

If they were not on time or did not give you a valid reason for tardiness, do not assume they will show up on time to work on your project or get it done on time.

The answer to these questions will probably determine how they will run your project.

One contractor went to check out a property a week after I had asked him. When he arrived, I already had another crew working full steam ahead. He got the point, and I gave him a second chance.

The next time I asked him for a bid, he knew I meant right away and was there the next day. We built a good relationship, and he ended up being one of the best contractors I have ever teamed up with.

WORKING WITH CONTRACTORS

When you know who you want to work with, do not be afraid to negotiate pricing. Be truly clear on payment arrangements, a completion date, and the scope of work via a contract.

Get everything in writing.

Make sure all specific details are covered in your contract, and do not sign it until you are completely satisfied with the terms.

I personally prefer to pay for finish materials while having contractors include rough materials in their pricing. Most contractors I have worked with prefer this as well. This allows me to have better control over the material budget while saving the contractors a little time and effort, which they appreciate.

Just make sure to have the materials ready when they need them.

Regarding rough materials, do a quick look at the website of your local home improvement store, or go to the store to see what items cost. This will allow you to notice if you are being overcharged.

Always protect your budget.

When dealing with contractors, communicate, communicate, communicate!

Communication is key for staying on schedule and budget.

Call for daily updates, stop by the worksite to do frequent inspections, and take plenty of pictures and notes.

Showing up and maintaining constant contact will prevent contractors from slacking off.

They can try this on other projects, but not yours!

Now, let us discuss payments.

First, never pay upfront and never pay in cash. You want a paper trail in case there are any disputes, as well as to manage your budget better.

Do not pay more than an initial 10% deposit, pay in advance for work that has not been completed, and never pay in full until the project is 100% *complete,* including inspections.

Before work even starts, get a W9 form filled out by contractors, if necessary, before you distribute your first check.

A W9 is a form required by the IRS if you pay independent contractors more than $600. (Please consult with your tax adviser.) Make sure the name on the W9 is the same as the name on the checks you write or to the account you transfer money into.

REI REMODEL TIP:

Never pay contractors for more than the completed work. However, also make sure not to hold up payments for work that is completed correctly either.

RECAP

- Do not rush into a contract with a contractor; take your time to select the right one for you.
- Communication is key; make your presence felt in a good way.
- Never pay in full until the project is 100% complete.

Contractor Worksheet

Contractor Information

Company and contractor name: Quality Construction - Don Smith

Business address: 50 Construction St, AnyCity, USA

Office phone: (123) 456-7890 Mobile: (123) 456-7890 Email: don@example.com

Website: www.example.com Lic# (if applicable): #1234567890

Years in business: 9 Number of projects completed: 43

Services provided: Quality Construction - Don Smith

Questions	Yes	No
Will the contractor provide customer references?	✓	
Will the contractor arrange for you to visit a current or completed project?		✓
Will the contractor have a dedicated crew working on your project?	✓	
Will workers be supervised?	✓	
Will the contractor provide daily updates?	✓	
Will the contractor obtain all necessary permits?	✓	
Will the contractor be able to start your project in a timely manner?	✓	
Will the contractor be able to complete your project in a timely manner?	✓	
Does the contractor have liability insurance?	✓	
Will the contractor provide you with a written contract?	✓	
Will the contractor provide a written lien waiver?	✓	
Will the contractor provide a written warranty for work performed?	✓	
Was the contractor responsive to your questions and concerns?	✓	
Did the contractor seem knowledgeable?	✓	
Do you think you could work well with this contractor?	✓	

Interview Notes

Don really knows his stuff. I scheduled him to look at the property.

3

FINAL BUDGET

The numbers will be your best friend
... do not take your eye off them!

We discussed the budget in the *Game Plan* section, and you will use that same form here.

The final budget is composed of actual numbers received from contractors—not your original "ballpark" figures.

The final budget will guide you through the management process by helping you keep costs under control and profits maximized!

Please remember to budget for unexpected costs by adding at least a 15% contingency. Remodeling can be unpredictable, and issues sometimes arise from what cannot be easily seen or accounted for.

RECAP

- Establish your budget, then stick to it.
- Include at least a 15% contingency for the unexpected.
- Focus the budget on items that will produce a greater return (kitchen and baths).

FINAL BUDGET

Project Budget Property: 1234 Remodel St.

Major Systems			
System	**Description**	**Ballpark $**	**Final $**
Septic System	NA	NA	NA
Sewer	Needs inspection	$300	$300
Roof	Good. Get roof cert from roofer	$150	$200
HVAC	Needs service. Upgrade thermostat.	$250	$500
Electrical Panel/ System	Upgrade	$3000	$2800
Water Heater	Replace existing	$800	$1000
Windows	Repair (2) windows	$300	$350
Plumbing System	Copper pipes in good shape	NA	NA
Foundation	No issues	NA	NA
Siding/ Stucco	Good shape	NA	NA
Chimney/ Fireplace	Functional	NA	NA
Crawlspace	No issues	NA	NA
Termite/ Pest Control	Exterminate roaches	$200	$175
Pool Spa	NA	NA	NA
Well	NA	NA	NA
Misc			

General Remodel			
Item	**Description**	**Ballpark $**	**Final $**
Lock Change/ Trashout	Change exterior locks. 40 yd trash out	$1650	$1875
Demo	Whole house. Need additional 40 yd dumpster	$2500	$2500
Framing/ Insulation	NA	NA	NA
Doors/ Windows	Replace (2)-32" int	$400	$350
Drywall	Patching throughout	$1950	$1750
Paint	Complete interior/ exterior	$9300	$9000
Kitchen	All new	$10,000	$13,400
Bathroom(s)	All new. (2) guest, (1) master	$18,000	$17,000

4

DESIGN SELECTIONS

Keep your design simple to appeal to a larger population of buyers.

You have completed your scope and budget. Now it is time to select the materials to install.

Revisit comps and review the ones with low DOM and ask yourself the following questions:

- Why did these properties sell faster than others?
- Are there unique features?
- Were they fully remodeled?

- How were the interior and exterior designed?
- Was it staged?

Checking comps is a good place to start, especially if you are not sure what level of remodel is necessary. You do not want to over-remodel for the neighborhood where your property is located, but you do not want to under-remodel either.

When choosing materials, I suggest going with medium-range selections, unless you are doing a higher-end remodel.

Stay away from cheap supplies.

You want to produce a quality product, and cheap items are often harder to install, have missing parts, and just will not last long term. However, you should be able to find quality items on clearance or on sale.

Many times, I have purchased products at economical prices that were of good quality.

Another cost-saving tip is to set up "pro" accounts with material suppliers for discounts and long-term savings. Many times, the more you purchase, the better the savings.

You have already established your budget, but see if you can come under it.

Money saved is money earned.

Order finish materials ahead of time so you do not lose time waiting. Even if you are not ordering special items and the home improvement store shows they have the stock, buy them ahead of time.

Several times I selected "in-stock" items that were out-of-stock when I went to purchase them.

REI REMODEL TIP: If you are ordering materials, always stay a step ahead of your contractors. Order items well in advance so you do not hold up the project.

I highly suggest you provide all contractors with what I call a *Materials Selection List* (see the example at the end of this chapter). This *Materials Selection List* outlines your design scheme and breaks down what materials go where.

We want to do our best to eliminate issues before they happen and prevent contractors from saying, "I thought this was to be installed here, not there!" (A phrase I have heard too many times before using *Materials Selection List*.)

Put your demolition plan into your *Materials Selection List* as well and *emphasize* what you will be keeping.

Using a design direction will help make your remodel go smoothly, but trust me, you will still need to make sure the design direction is being followed.

If you are new to design, here are some helpful pointers:

1. Keep it simple.
2. Pick a finish and stick to it throughout.
3. Choose durable products for rental properties.
4. Keep paint colors neutral.
5. Do light staging if you do not have the budget for a full stage (we will discuss staging later).

6. Hire a designer to design your remodel, or at least get a consultation.
7. A great design can be accomplished on any budget.

RECAP

- Keep it simple!
- Use the help of a designer if necessary.
- Do not over- or under-design your remodel.

Material Selections Property: 1234 Remodel St.

Room/ Area	Item	Description	Notes
(Kitchen)	(Tile Backsplash)	(Brand, style, color, model#, supplier)	(Install it on diagonal)
Kitchen	Paint	Behr Ultra, semi gloss, Swiss Coffee YL-W05, Home Depot	Paint walls only
Kitchen	Quartz Counters	Silestone, Quartz Calcutta Gold, QTZ-G9503, Quartz Warehouse	Install on both sides of island as well
Kitchen	Backsplash Tile	Satori, Hudson brilliant white 4x16 glossy, #1001-0201-0, Lowes	Install stacked on top of each other

5

PERMITTING

This process is not as daunting as you might think.

Trust me, permitting is not as daunting as it has been made out to be (depending on where you live, of course).

Seriously though, your contractors can pull the permits, or you can save money and gain control over this process by doing it yourself. It is not that difficult (no more contractors blaming the building department for delayed inspections!).

Some areas require plumbing, HVAC, and electrical contractors to pull permits for themselves, but you can still call the planning or building departments to confirm progress.

REI REMODEL TIP: Checking on your permit status *daily* might help speed up the process. Call the plan checker daily to check on your plans (as soon as phone calls are accepted). They will be more than willing to help speed up the process for you.

To confirm the code your building department uses, give them a call (or go online) to see what you need to submit to receive a permit. They likely already have templates ready for you to use and will gladly walk you through the process. They will even let you know what needs to be permitted and when you need to call for an inspection.

You will need to use an architect to draw plans for, let us say, an addition.

On the other hand, if you are keeping the same footprint and just moving some walls, light fixtures, or plumbing, you can sketch that up yourself, and your planning/building department may help walk you through the drawing.

Often, you can get simple permits the same day (i.e., fencing, patio cover, plumbing, electrical, HVAC, roofing, and simple remodels).

Major structural remodels or additions may take weeks depending on the department's workload, yet they should be able to give you an estimated timeline.

Even if you must wait on permits, find some work to start, get cabinets measured, demo started, etc.

You might ask yourself, "Why should I get the necessary permits?"

I have six answers for you:

1. They are required.
2. If you get caught doing unpermitted work, you will get a "Stop Work Order." You are now at the mercy of the building department. Your project will be halted until you get all the required permits, and it's possible that you will be required to demo the work already completed if you cannot show it was built to code. It is a

roll of the dice that many take. I prefer having more control over my project than that.

3. If you plan on selling your property, permits will help ease buyer's minds and not come back to haunt you in escrow to decrease your asking price, stall the sale, or possibly cancel the sale altogether.
4. Some lenders will refuse to lend to your buyers if there is unpermitted work.
5. You could receive fines.
6. Unpermitted work may not be included in appraisal values.

Do not risk paying to have work done that you might have to redo or that might not be appraised to add value to your property.

Getting inspections will also give you peace of mind that the work has been completed correctly.

So what needs to be permitted? Any major alteration or changes to your property footprint such as:

- Systems work like major plumbing, electrical, and HVAC
- Roofing
- Building walls
- Creating new doors/windows
- Foundations
- Patio covers

What items usually do not need permits? Simple projects like:

- Painting
- Replacing existing doors
- Flooring
- Countertops
- Replacing faucets
- Replacing light fixtures

Once you receive your permit, post it in a window at the front of the property, where it is visible to inspectors.

It is critical to make sure to call for inspection at each required stage and to make sure the completed work passes inspection before continuing the remodel.

RECAP

- Most large remodels will probably require permits, but check with your local building department to confirm what they require.
- It is *your* responsibility to ensure the proper permits are obtained.
- You can save money and have better control over the project if you decide to handle the permitting process. However, contractors know the process better and can save you time. You can still call and check in on the permits.

6

SCHEDULE

Schedule everything.

Your schedule is like a compass that will lead you in the right direction—but you must follow it.

Yes, a wrong step might be taken. Still, the schedule will allow you to adjust your course and answer the following questions:

- When will you need specific materials?
- When are payments due?
- Do you know when to schedule a lender inspection for a draw?

- How do you track progress?
- Most of all, when will you complete your project?

If you are using a GC, the GC will handle scheduling, but collaborate with him or her and check on the schedule often. Whether or not you are using a GC, you want a detailed schedule.

Are you managing and scheduling the project yourself?

Then you need to keep everyone in sync with your schedule, as if you are the conductor of a symphony.

If one contractor gets out of sync, it can derail the entire project, and that is not music to your ears!

Any deviations from the schedule must be dealt with, and adjustments must be made immediately. This is where having a list of backup contractors might come in handy.

Review the *Order of Work* list at the end of this chapter. It will show you what order to schedule work for your project. This is an order that works well for me.

However, you could adjust some items, and they may vary slightly per project.

Do what works best for your schedule.

REI REMODEL TIP: Use your contractors to help you put together the schedule.

Ask your contractors when they can start and how long it will take them to complete the job. You have an idea based on your initial interview.

Input that information into your calendar; I always add a day or two to the completion time they give. From there, continue down the *Order of Work* list until each task and contractor is scheduled.

Once you have completed a few projects, you will have an idea of the approximate length of each stage, and scheduling will become easier.

Keep at it; accuracy in scheduling comes with experience.

When you complete the schedule, break it down per day. For example, if your contractor says it will take three days to demo, ask what will be demoed each day. Then check every day to see if what they scheduled is happening.

This is a technique I use to encourage contractors to stick to my schedule. It is effective, especially if you show up on-site daily to check progress.

Continue down the list to schedule each contractor this way. This will help your contractors stay on track and give you a deeper insight into how to create a schedule.

You will catch delay issues in real time—not whenever the contractor chooses to tell you.

We would all love for every one of our projects to be flawless, but sometimes things happen out of our control. The weather may delay a roof installation, a delivery may come late, someone may become ill, et cetera—things we cannot forecast.

Even so, if changes to the schedule are required, communicate it and give a revised schedule to all necessary parties.

Keep moving forward!

Before starting a major remodel, do not forget to inform neighbors. Contact at least the neighbors on either side of your property, across the street, behind your property, and the neighbors to either side of those houses as well.

Reaching out will allow you to give them your contact information so they can contact you with any questions or alerts about your property. Instead of complaining to other neighbors or calling the city, they can call you.

Depending on the neighbors, you might get frequent calls, and this could become annoying. Despite this possible nuisance, communication is beneficial in avoiding problems with neighbors and in creating "allies" to help watch over your property.

Neighbors may also be helpful in spreading the word when you are ready to sell or rent your property.

In some cases, you might even find deals from a neighbor who wants to sell their house, or they might know another potential seller. The whole point here is to make friends, not enemies, and you can only do that by communicating.

RECAP

- Use your contractors to help you create a realistic schedule.
- Use the Order of Work list to correctly schedule contractors.
- Communicate and get to know the surrounding neighbors.

SCHEDULE

Order of Work

Step	Item	Notes
1	Demolition	
2	Foundation repairs	
3	Roof	
4	Framing and insulation	
5	Rough electrical, plumbing, and HVAC	
6	Windows	
7	Exterior repairs	
8	Drywall	
9	Doors and trim	
10	Tile in bathrooms	
11	Paint	
12	Flooring (other than carpet)	
13	Install baseboards	
14	Cabinets and counters	
15	Tile backsplash	
16	Finish electrical, plumbing, and HVAC	
17	Appliances	
18	Final install of finishes (shower door, accessories, etc.)	
19	Touch up paint	
20	Carpet	
21	Landscaping	
22	Cleaning/ haul debris	
23	Staging	
24	Pro photos	

Weekly Schedule

Week Start: Day/Month Property: 1234 Remodel St.

TIME	SUNDAY	MONDAY	TUESDAY	WEDNESDAY	THURSDAY	FRIDAY	SATURDAY
7:00 AM		Start Demo	Continue Demo	Exterior Prep	Start Plumbing	Start Drywall Patching	Drywall Patching
8:00 AM				Start Electrical			Bathrooms
9:00 AM							
10:00 AM							
11:00 AM				Exchange Dumpster		Start Bathroom Remodel	
12:00 PM					HVAC Service		
1:00 PM							
2:00 PM							
3:00 PM							
4:00 PM							
5:00 PM		End day	Finish Demo			Plumbing Done	
6:00 PM					Rough Electrical done		End day
7:00 PM							

PART 2

MID-REMODEL

The Mid-Remodel is where we carry out the game plan. You have put a lot of work into planning your remodel. Now it is time to manage performance to remain on schedule and on budget to maximize your profit.

7

MANAGEMENT TOOLS

Use the tools that work best for you.

The schedule you created is your main tool for managing a project, but a folder system and/or an online management system combined with your schedule gives you the power to increase efficiency and organization ten-fold.

I like to use both in combination with a free accounting app called Wave.

First, let us discuss the folder system. The folder is your key to keeping everything organized and accessible.

Before we get too deep into it, understand that this system is to be adapted to your personal circumstance and preference.

The folder system is simply a folder where you organize all your paperwork.

Start putting it together by printing out all the forms used in the *REI Remodel Process* and keep them handy in a three-ring binder with labeled dividers.

I usually manage several properties at a time, so I use a pocket divider for each project.

In this pocket divider, I store everything regarding a particular property. I also keep a duplicate file stored in my office filing cabinet and on my computer.

I do not like to admit it, but many times over the years, I was rushed and misplaced my folder.

Now, let us go digital with an online management system.

This is basically taking the schedule and putting it into a system like Trello, Asana, or your preferred software. Set calendar reminders for payments, progress evaluation, daily updates, inspections, etc.

I like that the online management system is another method to maintain communication with contractors.

I often add contractors to schedule reminders and keep all updates recorded in an online app.

The power in an online management system is the automated reminders, the ability to communicate and collaborate with contractors easily, and the ability to simply review the status of your project online from multiple devices.

Online accounting software is a good way to keep track of your budget. Some paid versions of project management software also do a good job at managing accounting.

Many options exist; however, I will just discuss free options that do a great job. Wave is one of them.

Use their mobile app to scan or input all receipts and use the name of your property to label all inputs. You can run multiple projects in one account, export accounting reports, and use it solely to track the financials of your projects.

RECAP

- Always use a management system to manage your remodel; choose the system that works best for you.
- Use automated reminders to stay on track.
- Accounting software is a great tool to manage your budget.

8

DAILY UPDATES AND TASKS

Stay up to date daily.

Now that you have your management system ready to go, it is time to stay on track with daily contractor updates or creating daily tasks if you are doing the project yourself. The goal now is to carry out all the hard work you put into the Pre-remodel stage.

Schedule a daily reminder to alert you to check on the day's progress so that you can adjust when necessary.

Unfortunately, issues are common in remodeling, and success usually depends on adjusting quickly.

You can now adjust because you have a well-thought-out plan, budget, and management system to follow.

REI REMODEL TIP: Visit your property at different times without letting contractors know you are stopping by to see how the project is being run when they are not expecting you.

Take frequent pictures, daily if possible. Have your contractor send you pictures on days you cannot visit your property.

What if daily tasks are not accomplished?

No, it is not the end of the world, but you will need to adjust your schedule. You could still hit your completion date, and that is what we are aiming for.

Remember, you created your schedule with some wiggle room. Unless you are performing every task yourself, you will need to prepare yourself to mitigate issues outside of your control.

You set yourself up for success by adding extra "just-in-case" days, creating a detailed budget, and making a list of backup contractors. When issues arise, complete a quick evaluation and then make the necessary adjustments.

RECAP

- Help keep your schedule on track with daily updates or tasks.
- Use your schedule to create daily tasks.
- Tracking daily tasks will help you adjust quickly.

Daily Updates/ Task Sheet

Property: 1234 Remodel St.

☐	Task	Notes
☐	Finished Demo	All demo is now complete and the 40yd bin needs replacement
☐	Ran wires for recessed lights	All wiring for recessed lighting is complete. Tomorrow, the panel will be upgraded.
☐		
☐		
☐		
☐		
☐		
☐		
☐		
☐		
☐		
☐		
☐		
☐		

Date: Day/Month

Summary of the day: ______________________________

____

____

9

PROGRESS EVALUATION

Keep your project on track!

Progress evaluation is exactly what it sounds like—evaluating or assessing the progress of your project.

Complete evaluations weekly.

You should have a good idea of where the project stands based on the implementation of daily updates and tasks. However, this is a more formal process where you will ask yourself first, and then your contractors, the questions included in the *Progress Evaluation* form.

The main items we will focus on are the schedule and budget.

Questions to ask yourself:

1. Is the project on budget? If so, can I do anything to save money? If not, why not, and what can be done to get back on budget?
2. Is the project on schedule? If yes, can I do anything to increase productivity? If not, what can be done to get back on schedule?

Questions to ask your contractor:

1. If the project is on schedule, does anything concern you about the schedule? Are there any areas where we could save time?
2. If the project is off schedule, how can we get back on schedule? Can I do anything to help us get back on schedule?
3. Whether you are on or off budget, are there any areas where we can save?

PROGRESS EVALUATION

Evaluate the current progress while continuing to think ahead. Anticipate the next steps and prepare for them.

Whenever meeting with contractors, approach them with a team mindset of collaboration and problem-solving.

Even if a contractor is running behind schedule, maintain focus on the objective, which is to complete your project in the most efficient way possible. This will help prevent contractors from taking offense and working against you.

I have had contractors work harder for me because I showed them respect.

Of course, this is not always the case.

In my experience, you may have to replace a contractor for not honoring his or her commitment to your contract. Because this is a possibility, make sure that the option to remove the contractor for non-performance is written in every contract you sign.

RECAP

- Do progress evaluations weekly with your contractors.
- Use the Progress Evaluation form to determine if you need to adjust your budget and schedule.
- Approach your contractors with a team mindset.

Progress Evaluation

Date: Day/ Month

Property: 1234 Remodel St.

Questions To Ask Yourself

1. Is the project on budget? If so, is there anything you can still do to save money? If not. Why not? What can be done to get back on budget?

   Yes. Instead of replacing the cabinets, we will change the doors and paint.

2. Is the project on schedule? If yes, is there anything I can do to increase productivity? If no, why not and what can be done to get back on schedule?

   No. There was a busted pipe in the wall behind the master shower. The schedule will need to overlap.

Questions To Ask Your Contractor

If the project is on schedule

1. Is there anything that concerns you about the schedule? Are there any areas where we could save time?

If the project is NOT on schedule

2. How can we get back on schedule? Is there anything I can do to help us get back on schedule?

   The plumbing contractor is bringing in another worker to help stay on schedule and the tile installer will start prepping the guest baths first.

Whether on or over budget

3. Are there any areas where we can save money?

   The busted pipe will cost extra but we're saving on the kitchen cabinets.

10

QUALITY CONTROL

Make sure it is done right!

Quality control is the process of monitoring work in progress and upon completion. You start this process by first discussing and agreeing upon the type of quality you require from your contractor.

Set these expectations before any work starts.

Review the *Quality Control* checklist with contractors and use this same checklist to monitor quality as your project progresses.

It is important to monitor quality throughout the project to cut down on wasted time, extra expenses, and effectively communicate your expectations to contractors as work unfolds.

Like I said before, communication is particularly important to get the results you desire.

Monitor the quality of labor and materials as often as possible, at every progress evaluation meeting, and before the start of a new phase of your remodel (I cannot emphasize this enough!).

Inspect work with a buyer's eye.

Keep in mind buyers can be critical, so if something pops out at you that just does not seem right, address it; a buyer will notice.

Quality control, as important as it is, is simple. Inspect work frequently, take pictures, and take notes about issues that need to be addressed. Look for issues such as:

- Over-sprayed or uneven paint
- Items painted that shouldn't be
- Uneven or crooked tile
- Noticeable drywall patches that do not blend in
- Damaged or low-quality materials that don't operate as they should

- Doors/windows/trim that aren't caulked
- Crooked cabinets or hardware
- Water leaks
- Doors or gates that do not close smoothly
- Squeaky subfloors
- Materials installed in the wrong location
- Materials used that were not in your design selections.

Remember to monitor quality throughout each stage of your remodel and once your contractor has completed the project.

At this point, many items should have already been addressed, but create a *Punch List* if necessary, to address any issues before final payment.

Use the *Scope Sheet* to help create your *Punch List.*

Issues may come up even after the remodel is "finished," such as a leak starting, a piece of tile coming loose, etc. These issues are common and will be covered by the warranty the contractor provides you.

Once the *Punch List* has been addressed, do a final walkthrough with your contractor.

Make sure all the items on the *Quality Control Checklist* are checked off and the scope is completed before handing over the final payment.

RECAP

- Use the Quality Control Checklist to help monitor quality.
- Inspect quality as often as possible and before progressing to a new stage of your remodel.
- Inspect with a buyer's eye.

QUALITY CONTROL

Quality Control Checklist

Property: 1234 Remodel St.

Yes	No	N/A	Answer Yes Or No To Each Of These Items
			Utilities
✓			Water is on
✓			Power is on
	✓		Gas is on
	✓		All gas appliances are lit (stove, water heater, etc)
			Exterior
			General
	✓		Doors open and close correctly
	✓		Paint is 100% complete (no peeling, mold, etc.)
✓			All stucco or siding is intact
	✓		Dry rot or termite damage has been replaced or repaired (fascia, eaves, etc.)
	✓		Exterior outlets are GFCI and enclosed in a waterproof housing
	✓		Exterior doors have weather stripping and thresholds installed correcty
✓			Doorbell works
✓			Mailbox is installed
	✓		Address numbers are installed and correct
✓			Exterior hose bibs do not leak and operate correctly
✓			Exterior lighting have bulbs and are operable
			Landscaping
	✓		Lawn sprinklers function correctly and are on an automatic timer
	✓		Landscaping is complete, grass is cut, and lawn maintenance is scheduled
✓			All fencing is upright and gates operate correctly
	✓		Trash bins are placed neatly inside garage or on the side of the house
	✓		All trash and remodeling materials have been hauled away
			Pool
		✓	Pool has been cleaned and is on a maintenance schedule
		✓	Pool equipment is in working condition (pump, filter, timer, light, and heater)
		✓	A GFCI plug has been installed for the pool equipment
		✓	Fencing and gates have been installed around the pool as needed
			Interior
			General
	✓		Smoke detectors are installed on each floor of the home, in every bedroom, and outside all sleeping areas
	✓		Carbon monoxide detectors are installed on each floor of the home, within 15 ft of each every bedroom
	✓		All light fixtures and ceiling fans are functioning correctly and have light bulbs installed

PART 3

POST-REMODEL

We are almost there! Your remodel is complete! But first, we must prepare the property to list. Complete the following Post-remodel steps to professionally prepare your property to sell or rent.

11

HOUSE PREP

Whether you are selling or leasing your property, follow these steps for a quicker exit.

CLEANING

Once your remodel is complete and the *Punch List* is done, it is time to clean everything up. Your remodeling contractor probably did a general cleanup, but now it is time to detail the property.

If you won't clean the property yourself, search for a cleaner as you did for your contractors. You will not need to interrogate them quite like you did your contractors, but ask the following questions:

1. Do you have experience doing after remodel cleanups?
2. What do you charge? (They probably have a method by which they charge (i.e., square footage, bed/baths, single/two-story, etc.)
3. What is your availability?

I suggest finding a cleaner while you are still remodeling and get them prepped and ready to go.

You want the house clean for potential buyers—but in this step—you are also getting it ready for the listing pictures.

Make sure everything on the interior of the house is wiped down, overspray paint is removed, excess grout or thinset is scraped up, windows are cleaned, carpets vacuumed, debris removed from cabinets, etc.

On the exterior of the property, immediately before pictures, I use the same landscaper I hire for lawn maintenance to complete tasks such as:

- Picking up all debris
- Picking weeds

- Cutting grass
- Power washing concrete
- Making sure all trash cans are behind a fence or placed neatly in the garage

RECAP
• Find cleaners before your remodel is done.

STAGING

Why?

After a thorough cleaning comes staging.

The first thing I want to say is, "Do not underestimate the value of staging!"

Whether you budgeted for light or full staging, I recommend you do not skip this step. Here is why…

Staging is remarkably effective in helping potential buyers visualize themselves in the home. Buying is an emotional experience, and staging will help set the mood, especially if you have awkward areas in your property.

Give a buyer an idea of what to do with the awkwardness.

Another plus is that buyers notice more flaws when a property is not staged.

Notice these stats:

1. According to realtor.com, on average, staged homes sell 88% faster and for 20% more than non-staged homes.
2. The average sell price of homes is a reduction of 10–20% from the asking price. Whereas staged homes, according to Coldwell Banker, sell for over 6% above the asking price.
3. The National Association of Realtors states that every $100 invested in staging gives a potential return of $400.

These stats are significant, right?

Even so, the initial sticker shock of staging fees deters sellers from committing to do it.

From an investor/ business point of view, this is a no-brainer and should be accounted for.

Cost

So how much does staging cost?

Surely it depends on where your house is located, but to get your home professionally staged might cost around $500 per room, plus a total monthly fee of around $500.

If you would like to use your own furniture, you could probably find a designer to stage for less than $1,000. You could also do light staging yourself from $150 to $500.

Tips

There are a few ways to stage. You can stage every room with all the furniture and accessories, or you can save money and only stage key areas like the master bed, living room, kitchen, dining room, and awkward spaces.

You might even want to stage an outdoor space, especially if it is small, to display its potential.

I suggest using a designer to help you with full staging.

For light staging, you can build your own staging kit. Focus on the kitchen and bathrooms and use accessories in areas that would look good accented.

No matter who does the staging, keep the design neutral and make sure it fits the style of your house (i.e., no traditional staging for a modern house).

Follow these simple recommendations:

1. Keep it neutral.
2. Remove personal items.
3. Declutter.
4. Clearly define spaces.

RECAP

- Plan and budget to stage your property.
- Do a full stage if possible, but follow the light staging checklist to stage your property yourself.
- Staging helps you sell your property faster for more money.

PROFESSIONAL PICTURES

Once staging is done, get professional pictures taken of your property. You have come all this way with a top-notch remodel, cleaning, and staging, so do not skimp now.

HD pictures will set your property apart from other properties and will properly showcase all the hard work put into your property. And yes, opt for the aerial drone shot, as well. You might even want to consider a virtual 3D home tour.

Your realtor can probably give you a good referral for a photographer.

You are almost there; finish strong!

If you want to commit to taking your own photos, buy a good DSLR or mirrorless camera that is within your budget and follow these basic tips:

1. Take wide-angle pictures.
2. Take your pictures when there is plenty of natural light; open blinds/curtains; turn on all lights; and make sure all the pictures have consistent lighting.

3. Prepare each room beforehand.
4. Find creative angles to shoot.
5. Use a tripod.
6. Test out different exposures.
7. Take several pictures of each space.
8. Use ND filters for exterior shots.

On the one hand, you could save money by learning how to take pictures yourself, and you will no longer have to worry about scheduling or receiving pictures on time from a photographer.

On the other hand, getting professional pictures does not take too much away from your budget and will save you time.

You decide what works better for you.

RECAP

- Take HD pictures of your property. Hire a photographer or take them yourself.

12

LISTING INFORMATION

Use the improvements you have completed to market your property.

Use the *Listing Information* form to gather information during your project. This will streamline giving information to your realtor.

Have it ready beforehand and document improvements that will be marketed to sell your property.

Also, gather your material selections along with necessary product information and warranties for installed items.

RECAP

- Gather information about your property throughout your remodel.

Listing Information

Property Details

Address: 1234 Remodel St.

Bed/Bath: 4/3 SqFt House/Lot: 2300/ 12300 Year Built: 1983

Other: HOA - Remodel Street HOA, contact Mary (123) 456-7890

List of Improvements

- Int/ext paint
- New bathrooms
- Upgraded kitchen
- New carpet
- New waterproof laminate
- New Quartz counters in kitchen
- New plumbing fixtures
- New electrical fixtures

Listing Notes *(Special features of the property, etc)*

This property has a nook off the kitchen that would be great for additional working space. There is also great mountain views from the master bedroom.

Appliances

- SS stove
- SS dishwasher
- SS Microwave

Utilities

- Natural gas
- Electrical
- City water/ sewer

Certifications

- Roof cert
- Sewer inspection
- Foundation report

Notes:

13

HOUSE MAINTENANCE

Keep your property looking good!

You want to make sure your property is well-maintained and shows well anytime a buyer stops by, so schedule regular lawn maintenance and refresh cleanings.

A refresh cleaning will cost less than a full remodel cleaning. It is a fresh wipe down of surfaces on the interior and quick sweep up of debris on the exterior.

You or your realtor could easily do this yourselves.

Complete these items before weekends.

Also, keep in mind the way your property smells and address any foul odors. Remember to maintain a buyer's eye (and nose) to catch any issues before buyers do.

RECAP

- Schedule maintenance to keep your property showing well.

14

FINAL THOUGHTS

Well done. Now on to the next one!

So, that is it!

Not that complicated, right?

You have gone through the entire *REI Remodel Process* and now have insight into how to plan, manage, and complete a profitable rei remodel.

I would love to hear from you, see pictures, and help you along with your remodel. Reach out to me if you have any questions at dc@reiremodel.com or on Instagram at @reiremodel.

Need a little more assistance? Visit us at www.reiremodel.com to schedule a free consultation.

15

BONUS—REMODEL SUSTAINABLY

A little goes a long way.

I believe in being a good steward of our environment and deplore throwing away perfectly good items. So while demoing, I like to upcycle and keep as many items out of the landfill as possible, sometimes making a few bucks along the way.

I am sure you know the phrase, "One person's trash is another person's treasure." Well, it is true.

When you demo, salvage what you can, and then sell it, give it away, or do a mixture of both. Trust me—someone can and will use it.

Many times, I removed perfectly built (but dated) cabinets, put them on craigslist, and sold them during a remodel. Other times I put items on the curb or gave them to workers.

You can also be sustainable by using products with recycled items in them. Wood, bamboo, cork, and steel are all sustainable materials that you may incorporate into your remodel.

Use water-efficient fixtures, LED lighting, and eco-friendly paint. Some of these items are now required under California's "Building Energy Efficiency Standards."

You may also create a landscape that does not consume too much water.

Right now, a completely sustainable remodel is more expensive and might not be feasible for your investment project. Nevertheless, these are some tips to help you incorporate what you can.

Eventually, pricing will come down as sustainability becomes more widespread. Something is better than nothing!

RECAP

- The best way to start remodeling sustainably is to upcycle items that you demo.
- Use sustainable materials.
- Install a landscape that does not need a lot of water.

www.ingramcontent.com/pod-product-compliance
Lightning Source LLC
La Vergne TN
LVHW051013080826
845145LV00009B/2605